Google Pixel

9 & 9 Pro

User Guide

The Step-By-Step Instruction Manual To Unlocking Google Pixel 9 & 9 Pro Features For Beginners & Seniors, With Tips & Tricks To Master Your Smartphone Experience

By

Max S. Brown

Copyright © Max S. Brown.

Table of Contents

INTRODUCTION

The launch of the new Pixel 9 Pro XL marks the first time Google's Pixel Pro series offers two sizes. The XL label denotes that the Pixel 9 Pro XL has a huge screen, although it is around the same size as previous Pixel Pro phones, if somewhat larger. The Pixel 9 Pro stands out from previous Pixel Pros by having a smaller display.

All of Google's new phones use the company's latest CPU, the Tensor G4, and have much more RAM than prior generations to power Google's new AI features.

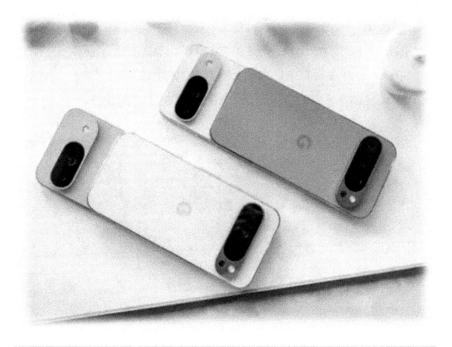

All new Pixel 9 phones, including the base model, have Google's super-bright Actua panels, which debuted with the Pixel 8 Pro in 2023. From the start, the processor and display combo worked flawlessly: all Pixel 9 phones ran smoothly and rapidly, and the panels were very brilliant, giving deep, rich colors and contrast.

The Pixel 9 series screens have a new ultrasonic fingerprint sensor, which should enable faster and more accurate unlocking.

Google's new Pixel 9 series is a total redesign of the Pixel 8 series, and it looks and feels like a new generation. The corners are now flat, as seen on Apple and Samsung's most current phones, and the distinctive Pixel camera module on the back is now a raised oval that spans the whole of the phone, rather than a bar that blends into the sides.

The base Pixel 9 features a clear glass back with a frost-textured aluminum frame, whilst the Pixel 9 Pro variants have the reverse: a frost-textured back with a shiny polished metal frame.

The Pixel 9 Pro is the smallest Pixel Pro model yet, with a 6.3-inch display that is the same size as the original Pixel 9. The Pixel 9 Pro XL features a 6.8-inch display, which is 0.1 inch larger than the Pixel 8 Pro, making it the largest Pixel Pro model to date.

The Pixel 9 and Pixel 9 Pro have identical 6.3-inch displays, while the Pixel 9 Pro has a 6.8-inch screen.

As with previous Pixel generations, only the Pro models have a triple-lens camera system, whereas the base model has a dual-lens camera. The Pro models also have a far better front camera, with more megapixels and a broader field of view than the base model.

Features of Google Pixel 9

	Pixel 9	Pixel 9 Pro	Pixel 9 Pro XL
Display	6.3-inch OLED, 1,080 x 2,424 resolution, 422 PPI, 60-120Hz refresh rate, 20:9 aspect ratio, 2,700 nits peak brightness	6.3-inch LTPO OLED, 1,280 x 2,856 resolution, 495 PPI, 1-120Hz refresh rate, 20:9 aspect ratio, 3,000 nits peak brightness	6.8-inch LTPO OLED, 1,344 x 2,992 resolution, 486 PPI, 1-120Hz refresh rate, 20:9 aspect ratio, 3,000 nits peak brightness
Processor	Tensor G4	Tensor G4	Tensor G4
RAM	12GB	16GB	16GB
Storage	128GB / 256GB	128GB / 256GB / 512GB / 1TB	128GB / 256GB / 512GB / 1TB
Battery	4,700mAh	4,700mAh	5,060mAh
Power	27W wired charging Wireless charging Battery Share	27W wired charging Wireless charging Battery Share	37W wired charging Wireless charging Battery Share
Cameras	Rear: - 50MP wide camera, f/1.68, 82-degree FoV, 1/1.31" sensor - 48MP ultrawide camera, f/1.7, 123-degree FoV, 1/2.55" sensor Front: 10.5MP, f/2.2, 95-degree FoV	Rear: - 50MP wide camera, f/1.68, 82-degree FoV, 1/1.31" sensor - 48MP ultrawide camera, f/1.7, 123-degree FoV, 1/2.55" sensor - 48MP telephoto camera, f/2.8, 22-degree FoV, 5x optical zoom, 1/2.55" sensor Front: 42MP, f/2.2, 103-degree FoV	Rear: - 50MP wide camera, f/1.68, 82-degree FoV, 1/1.31" sensor - 48MP ultrawide camera, f/1.7, 123-degree FoV, 1/2.55" sensor - 48MP telephoto camera, f/2.8, 22-degree FoV, 5x optical zoom, 1/2.55" sensor Front: 42MP, f/2.2, 103-degree FoV

Connectivity	5G (mmWave + Sub6) Wi-Fi 7 (802.11/be) Bluetooth 5.3 (dual antenna)	5G (mmWave + Sub6) Wi-Fi 7 (802.11/be) Bluetooth 5.3 (dual antenna) Ultra-wideband chip	5G (mmWave + Sub6) Wi-Fi 7 (802.11/be) Bluetooth 5.3 (dual antenna) Ultra-wideband chip
SIM	Dual SIM (Single Nano SIM and eSIM)	Dual SIM (Single Nano SIM and eSIM)	Dual SIM (Single Nano SIM and eSIM)
Security	Face Unlock (Class 3) Ultrasonic under-display fingerprint sensor Titan M2 chip	Face Unlock (Class 3) Ultrasonic under-display fingerprint sensor Titan M2 chip	Face Unlock (Class 3) Ultrasonic under-display fingerprint sensor Titan M2 chip
Durability	IP68 Gorilla Glass Victus 2	IP68 Gorilla Glass Victus 2	IP68 Gorilla Glass Victus 2
Software	Android 14 7 years of OS, security, and Pixel Drop updates	Android 14 7 years of OS, security, and Pixel Drop updates	Android 14 7 years of OS, security, and Pixel Drop updates
Dimensions and weight	152.8 x 72.0 x 8.5mm 198g	152.8 x 72.0 x 8.5mm 199g	162.8 x 76.6 x 8.5mm 221g
Colors	Obsidian Porcelain Wintergreen Peony	Obsidian Porcelain Hazel Rose Quartz	Obsidian Porcelain Hazel Rose Quartz

Camera

Since the Pixel series is all about photography, let us begin with the camera situation. Pixel phones are commonly considered as some of the greatest cameras money can buy.

The base model has a 50MP primary camera with Octa PD, an auto-focus technology used on big sensors to achieve great sensitivity and resolution. It shares the Pixel 8's aperture (f/1.68), field of vision (82 degrees), and sensor size (1/1.31). Furthermore, the front camera, which features a 10.5MP lens, is carried over from the previous year's model. The ultrawide has been increased from 12MP to 48MP. This ultrawide lens has an aperture of f/1.7, a field of view of 123 degrees, and a sensor size of 1/2.55 inch.

The Pixel 9 Pro has always had a triple camera configuration. The arrangement retains the main and ultrawide cameras from the entry model but adds a 48MP telephoto with a $f/2.8$ aperture, a 22-degree field of view, and a 1/2.55-inch sensor. However, we do get an upgraded front camera. The Pixel 9 Pro has a 42MP front camera with a $f/2.2$ aperture and a 103-degree ultrawide field of view, compared to the Pixel 8 Pro's 10.5MP. The Pro XL has the same camera equipment as the Pixel 9 Pro.

Performance

The Pixel 9 series features Google's latest CPU, Tensor G4. If all goes as planned, this will very likely be the final Tensor chipset, based on Samsung's Exynos architecture.

Tensor G4 boosts overall performance. Web browsing is 20% faster, app launches are 17% faster, and the phone performs better for routine tasks like snapping photos or streaming content.

To accomplish these accomplishments, the chip has been enhanced with several capabilities, including the new Samsung Modem 5400. This modem is faster and more efficient than the Samsung Modem 5300 in the Pixel 8 series. Furthermore, the Tensor

G4 has a more typical 4+3+1 configuration than the Tensor G3, as well as newer Arm ARMv9.2 cores (Cortex-A520, Cortex-A720, and Cortex-X4). These changes were designed to keep the device running cool and boost performance.

Moving on to RAM and storage, RAM capacity has increased. The storage of Pixel 9 is 128GB or 256GB but with 12GB of RAM. The Pixel 9 Pro and Pro XL feature 16GB of RAM and storage options ranging from 128GB to 1TB.

Screen Quality and Size

The Pixel 9 series is slightly larger than the previous generation, allowing Google to use larger displays this time.

The Pixel 9 and Pixel 9 Pro have many similarities, but the display is one area where they differ. The Pixel 9's OLED screen has expanded by 0.1 inch since last year, reaching 6.3 inches. This Actua panel has a pixel density of 422 PPI, a resolution of 2,424 x 1,080, and a refresh rate of 60-120Hz. Aside from the refresh rate, which remains constant, all of them are enhancements over previous versions. It also increases brightness to a maximum of 2,700 nits.

The Pixel 9 Pro also boasts a 6.3-inch OLED display, however, it's an LTPO Super Actua panel. This implies that Google's phone can reach extraordinary brightness — up to 3,000 nits — without sacrificing color vibrancy or clarity. It may also reduce its 120Hz frame rate to 1Hz when viewing static material, which can assist extend battery life.

Meanwhile, the Pixel 9 Pro XL stands out for its 6.8-inch OLED LTPO Super Actua display. Interestingly, this panel has a lesser pixel density than the Pro model, at 486 PPI. However, the difference is unlikely to be noticeable, particularly given the panel's higher resolution of 2,992 x 1,344. It offers 3,000 nits of brightness, similar to the Pro, and a refresh rate of up to 120Hz but as low as 1Hz.

The new Pixel family features the same 20:9 aspect ratio as the 2023 generation.

Design, colors, and build quality

This year, Google made the most substantial design changes to the Pixel. The 2024 model replaces the handset's camera bar, which has been a defining element of the series, with an oval-shaped camera pill. Furthermore, the squared-off edges of earlier generations have been changed with a more curved design comparable to the Pixel 8a.

The basic and Pro variants are somewhat taller, broader, and thinner than the Pixel 8, measuring 152.8 x 72.0 x 8.5 mm. This also suggests that the Pro version is smaller, thinner, and less thick than the Pixel 8 Pro. The Pixel 8 Pro and Pixel 9 Pro XL have nearly identical dimensions: 162.8 x 76.6 x 8.5mm.

Meanwhile, the flat display and Gorilla Glass return. The two most noticeable distinctions between this year's and previous year's panels are the increased screen sizes and the usage of Gorilla Glass Victus 2 throughout the line. The Pixel 9 and 9 Pro now have 6.3-inch screens, while the Pro XL has 6.8.

Moving on to build quality, the hardware has Gorilla Glass Victus 2 on the front and back. The vanilla model's glass has a polished finish, whereas the 9 Pro and Pro XL feature a smooth matte finish. You should also expect an IP68 water and dust-resistant rating.

In terms of colors, Google has added a new choice for all three models, bringing the total number of colorways to 4. Each model will get Obsidian (black) and Porcelain (white), along with a few model-specific colors. The Pixel 9 will replace last year's Rose (dull pink) and Hazel (light gray/greenish) with Wintergreen (light green) and Peony (reddish pink). Meanwhile, the Pro and Pro XL have lost Bay (blue) while gaining Hazel and Rose Quartz (light pink).

Battery life and charging speed

Beginning with the Pixel 9, Google endowed its entry-level smartphone with a 4,700mAh battery. This indicates that the Pixel 9 has 125mAh more battery capacity than the Pixel 8 (4,575mAh). While seeing an increase is encouraging, there is unlikely to be a major change in real life. In terms of charging, Google continues to play it safe, offering a 27W charging speed that can bring you up to 55% full in 30 minutes.

The Pixel 9 Pro arrives next, and it is slightly downgraded. The Pro, like the standard model, has a battery capacity of 4,700mAh, down from 5,050mAh last year. This is most likely because the Pro and Vanilla versions have identical sizes. Furthermore, the device features a charging speed of 27W.

The 9 Pro XL has a slightly larger battery (5,060mAh). With a charging rate of 37W, this Pixel may be the one you've been looking for. Google states that your battery can regain 70% of its charge in 30 minutes.

All three models are 12W Qi-certified, so your wireless charger will still work. The second-generation Pixel Stand supports 15W wireless charging on the Pixel 9, 21W on the Pixel 9 Pro, and 23W on the Pixel 9 Pro XL.

Battery Share is also back, allowing you to charge other devices using your phone's battery, including the recently introduced Pixel Buds Pro 2.

Software and Updates

Pixel 9 series will run Android 14. Regarding Google's update commitment, each Pixel 9 model will receive seven years of operating system, security, and feature updates.

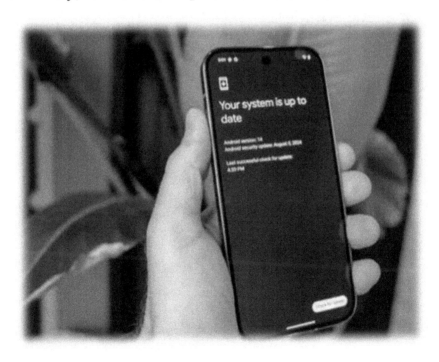

How to Set Up Your Device

Setting up a Google Pixel smartphone, or even an Android device, for the first time can be scary. But don't worry, we've got you covered. Let's begin by going over the Google Pixel setup process.

The first thing you must do is turn on your smartphone. The power button is placed on the phone's right side, above the volume rocker. Once the display turns on and a bright white screen with the Google logo shows, hold down the power button for a few seconds.

You will be greeted with a "Welcome to your Pixel" screen once you have passed the bootup process. This page allows you to select your phone's language as well as whether you want to enable Assistive features. You may alter the Vision settings and also set up the phone with your voice using the assistive options. You may also use touch to configure the phone by tapping "Get Started" in the lower right-hand area.

If you do not have a SIM card in your phone, you will be prompted to connect to a mobile network. When you sign up for cellular service, your wireless provider will usually supply you with a SIM card. You may need to transfer this from your old phone to the Google Pixel. If you are unfamiliar, you can refer to our guide. Simply locate the SIM slot and eject it with a SIM ejection tool, paperclip, or other similar instrument. If you do not have a physical SIM card, you may be able to work with your cellular carrier to obtain an eSIM.

If you do not have a data connection, the phone will prompt you to connect to a Wi-Fi network to complete the setup. Once you've established a connection, the phone will begin preparing your phone.

When the process is complete, you will be invited to either copy your apps and data or skip the process.

If you wish to not transfer any data from your old phone, you can skip this step.

If you want to transfer your data, you can do it from an iPhone or another Android phone.

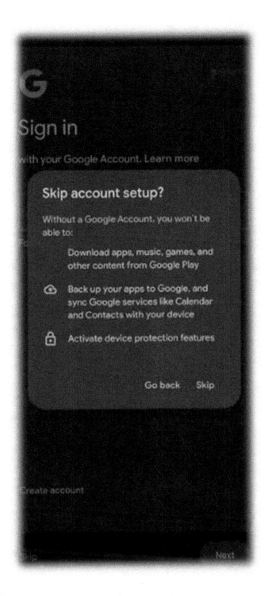

You will next be prompted to configure Google Services that you intend to use. Location settings, Wi-Fi scanning settings, providing diagnostic data, and other choices will be available. Examine each option carefully before making your choice. When you are pleased with your options, click "Accept." Following that, you must agree to some more legal terms to proceed.

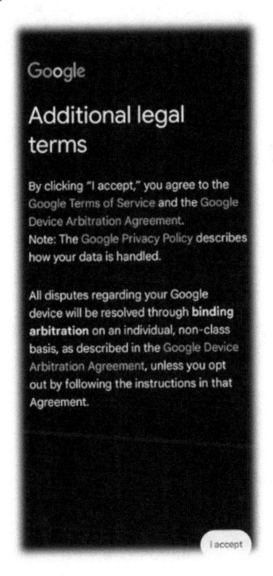

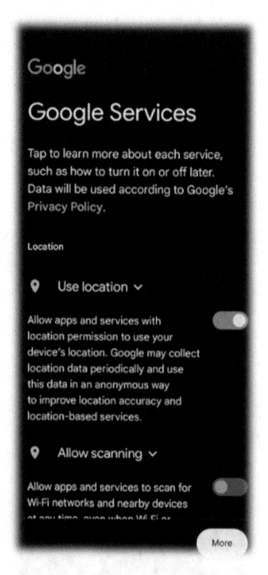

At this point, you will be able to set up a security code for your lock screen. When you click "Screen lock options," you can also enter a pattern, password, or PIN in addition to the four-digit PIN that is entered by default. This step is optional, however, if you choose to enter a security code, you will be asked to do it again.

If you input a security code, you will be asked to register a fingerprint to effortlessly unlock your smartphone. You can accept the process by tapping I Agree or avoid it by tapping No Thanks. Next, you'll be given the choice to install additional Google apps; if you do, select Ok; otherwise, uncheck the box next to "All of the following apps."

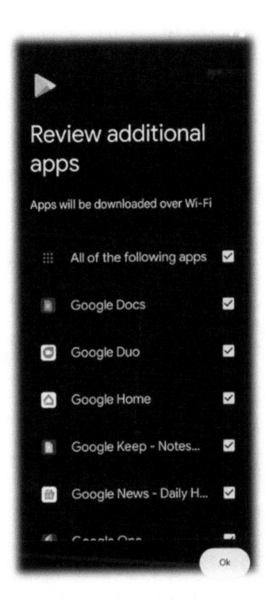

Finally, you will be given instructions on how to use the phone. Select Try it if you want a tutorial on gesture navigation, or else Skip. That's it, you've finished the setup process. Swiping up will bring you to your Google Pixel default home screen.

Basic Settings

How to turn off or restart your device

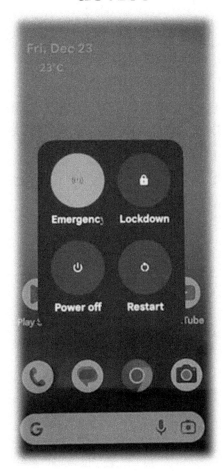

Switch off the Pixel using the button combo

Follow these simple methods to instantly turn off your Google Pixel:

1) Locate the volume down and side buttons as follows:
2) The side button is the small button above the bigger volume button.
3) The volume button is the lengthy button on the right side of the phone when the screen is facing you. The volume down button is found at the bottom of this long button.
4) Keep them together for 3-5 seconds. This will open the power menu on your screen.
5) To switch off the device, press the Power off button on the screen, or to restart it, press the Restart button.

Remapping the side key to open the power menu

Simply follow the steps listed below:

1) Navigate to Settings > System > Gestures. Keep the power button pressed.
2) Select the Power menu option from the Press and hold the power button to access the area. The

default Digital Assistant option will be replaced by the Power menu options.

3) When you long-press the Side key on your Pixel, the power menu will appear.

Make use of the quick settings menu.

If you don't want to memorize the button combination, Google has included a power menu shortcut under the Quick Settings menu.

1) To uncover the notification shade, swipe down once on your home screen. Swipe down again to bring up the Quick Settings menu.
2) A power icon appears in the bottom right corner.
3) Tap the power icon to open the power menu.

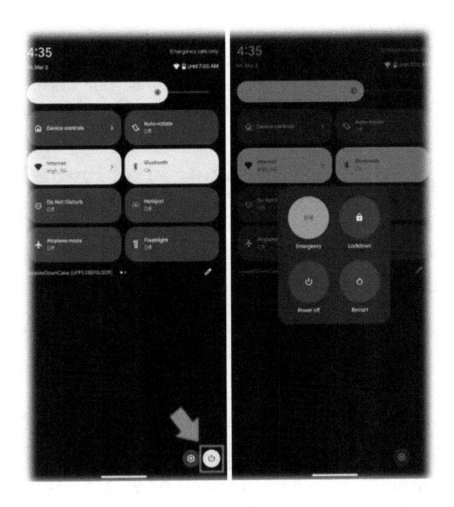

How to Use Google Assistant to turn the phone off

Google Assistant can also launch the Pixel's power menu for you.

1) To activate Google Assistant, tap the Side key or speak "Hey Google", which is the default wake word.

2) Use phrases such as "Turn off my phone," "Switch off," or "Restart my phone."

3) When Google Assistant recognizes your voice, it displays the power menu. You can use the turn-off or restart buttons according to your needs.

How to Charge Your Pixel Phone

All Pixel phones support charging through USB-C cables. Use the power adaptor that comes with some phones for the greatest results.

How to charge your phone

1) Attach the USB-C cable's two ends to your phone's bottom connector.

2) Attach the other end of the cord to the phone's included power adapter.

3) Attach the power adapter to an electrical outlet.

How to use Adaptive Charging

Adaptive Charging may activate to charge your phone to 100% one hour before you disconnect it if you charge it for an extended amount of time or overnight. The Adaptive Charging function helps your battery last longer.

Adaptive preferences

Adaptive Charging

Extend battery lifespan by charging steadily during longer charging periods. Activated based on your usage cycle.

Adaptive Battery

Extend battery life based on your phone usage

To extend battery life, Adaptive Battery may reduce performance and background activity. Some notifications may be delayed.

One feature that picks up on your charging patterns is called Adaptive Charging. If a long charging session is planned, it might still turn on in addition to the previously mentioned circumstances.

Follow these steps to turn off adaptive charging:

1) Launch the Settings app on your phone.

2) Choose Battery and then Adaptive Charging.

3) Stop the Adaptive Charging feature.

4) You'll get a notification letting you know when your battery will be fully charged once you enable adaptive charging.

5) Tips for Charging: How to Charge Fast

6) Use a wall outlet to supply electricity. For instance, laptop computers may charge more slowly.

7) While your phone is charging, you can use it. To expedite the charging process, do not use it while it is charging.

8) When your phone is charging, you can hear it.

Verify that your phone's ringtone is activated.

1) Launch the Settings app on your phone.

2) Select Sound, followed by Advanced.

3) Select the Charging Sound option.

4) There will be a sound when your phone is plugged in.

5) You won't hear anything if your phone is silent or vibrating.

How to get a SIM & add it to your Pixel phone

You can use an active nano SIM card or eSIM to connect your phone to a mobile network. If you don't have one, you'll get a "No SIM card" notice.

Use a nano SIM card

To obtain a nano SIM card, contact your cell service provider.

You can utilize the nano SIM card in your current phone instead of getting a new one.

Make use of eSIM.

Put in your SIM card.

With your phone switched off:

Insert the SIM ejection tool into the little hole on the left edge of the phone.

Push softly but firmly until the tray pops out.

Insert the nano SIM card after removing the tray.

Gently push the tray back into its slot.

You may need to restart your phone to get mobile service. To restart an active phone, press and hold the power button for approximately three seconds. Then choose Restart.

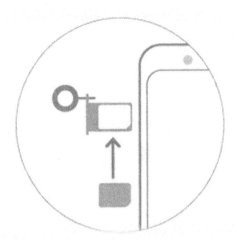

How to Change wallpaper on your Pixel phone

You may change the background visuals on your phone's Home and lock screens. You can utilize your phone's pictures or photos, even ones that update automatically.

1) Touch and hold an empty spot on the Home screen of your phone.
2) Choose your wallpaper and style. If you don't see "Wallpaper & Style," check for it in Wallpapers.
3) Change the wallpaper.
4) To use your image, select My Photos.
5) Select a category and then an image to use a curated image.
6) Choose Living Universe or Bloom to use a live wallpaper. Click Download if needed.

7) Choose Set wallpaper or Done from the bottom options.
8) Select the screen or screens that the wallpaper should appear on, if any.

How to add special effects to photo wallpapers

1) On your phone's Home screen, touch and hold an empty area.
2) Tap Wallpaper, then My Photos.
3) Select an image.
4) Choose Effects.

Enable the Create Cinematic wallpaper option.

1) Go to the Home screen, then the Lock screen, to see a sample of your wallpaper.
2) You can select where you want your wallpaper to appear by tapping the Home, Lock, or both screens.

How to Create custom wallpapers
Choose an emoji or a random choice:

1) Press and hold the empty area on your phone's Home screen.
2) Select Emoji Workshop, Wallpaper Change, and Wallpaper & Style.

3) Tap Edit Emoji, then Done in the bottom right corner.
4) Select an emoji.
5) Use the keyboard to find a specific emoji. Up to 14 emojis can be used to create your background.
6) Tap Randomize to get a random assortment.

Choose a size and pattern:

1) Select Patterns from the bottom panel.
2) Decide on the pattern style.
3) Use the slider to adjust the emoji's size on the pattern.

Select a color:

1) In the bottom panel, select Colors.
2) Select a background color.

Preview and configure your wallpaper:

To see an example of your emoji wallpaper, go to the Lock screen, then the Home screen.

1) When your preview is finished, click Set wallpaper.
2) Tap the Home screen or the Home and Lock screens to adjust the wallpaper's position.

How to Create AI Wallpapers

Using your suggestions, generative AI can produce original and distinctive wallpapers. You could:

1) Use the current wallpaper settings to see the new wallpaper.
2) To create a prompt, fill in the blanks in a prewritten template.
3) Choose a variety of options to fine-tune the final effect.
4) Save produced wallpapers for later use.
5) To create an AI wallpaper, follow these steps:
6) Tap and hold an empty spot on the Home screen of your phone.
7) Then, select Wallpaper and Style, More Wallpapers, and lastly AI Wallpaper.
8) Choose a theme for your AI-generated wallpaper.
9) Tap Inspire me to get a random wallpaper for the prompt you've selected.
10) Click on any highlighted word in the prompt to look up particular possibilities.
11) Tap Create wallpaper to start creating a wallpaper.
12) Use your left or right swipe to browse through wallpapers created by AI.

13) Select Done, then Lock or Home screen, and finally To alter the wallpaper, select a different one.

14) When you use a wallpaper, it is saved for future use.

Change the appearance of your home screen.

To alter the fonts, icons, shapes, and colors on your Home screen, adhere to these guidelines.

1) Press and hold an empty spot on your phone's Home screen.
2) Select Wallpaper & Style.
3) Select Wallpaper or Basic colors.
4) Choose a look.
5) Select Apply or Done.

Change the Home screen grid

You can adjust the grid's size on your Home screen by doing the following:

1) Press and hold an empty spot on your phone's Home screen.
2) Decide on your style and wallpaper.
3) Tap the App grid at the bottom.
4) Select a grid size.
5) Select done

Make use of themed icons.

Follow these instructions to change the color scheme of supported app icons:

1) Press and hold an empty spot on your phone's Home screen.
2) Select Wallpaper & Style.
3) Toggle the Themed icons on or off at the bottom.

How to add apps, shortcuts & widgets to your Home screens

You may customize your Home screens to easily access your favorite stuff.

How to Add to Home Screens

Add an app

1) From the bottom of your Home screen, swipe up.
2) Drag your finger across the app. An image represents each Home screen.
3) Move the app to the desired area by swiping it. Raise one of your index fingers.

Add a shortcut

1) After touching and holding the app, lift your finger. If the program supports shortcuts, you'll see a list of them.
2) Maintain your finger on the shortcut.

3) Move the shortcut to the desired location by dragging it. Raise one of your index fingers.
4) Tap a shortcut to use it without adding it to your home screen.

How to Add or resize a widget
Add a widget

1) Place your finger on an empty spot on the Home screen.
2) Select Widgets
3) Locate the app that has the desired widget in it.
4) Tap the app to get a list of widgets that are compatible with it.
5) Examine the device that you are holding. Pictures of your Home screens will appear.
6) Swipe the widget to move it to the desired location. Raise one of your index fingers.
7) Widgets are included in some apps. Maintain your finger on the app. Then choose Widgets.

Resize a widget

1) Hold your finger over the widget on the Home screen.
2) Lift your index finger. If the widget can be enlarged, an outline with dots on the sides will show.
3) Drag the dots to adjust the widget's size.

4) Press outside the widget once you're finished.

How to Organize Your Home Screens

Create a folder (group).

1) Press and hold a shortcut or app.
2) Place one shortcut or app on top of another. Lift a single index finger.
3) Drag each new addition to the group's top to add it.
4) Tap the group to give it a new name. Next, press the recommended folder name. In addition, you can choose a suggested name from the list at the top of the keyboard or type your own.

Move an app, shortcut, widget, or group

1) Drag your finger across the item. Pictures of your Home screens will appear.
2) Move the item to the desired spot by swiping it.
3) Raise one of your index fingers.

Remove an app, shortcut, widget, or group

1) Hold the app
2) Remove the object by dragging it up.
3) Raise your index finger.

4) "Remove," "Uninstall," or both options are available. "Remove" just removes an app from your Home screen. "Uninstall" removes it from your device.

Add a Home screen

1) Take hold of the application, shortcut, or group.
2) Drag it to the right until the Home screen disappears.
3) Lift your index finger.

Remove a Home screen

Delete the apps, groups, widgets, and shortcuts from your home screen.

1) The Home screen will disappear after the last screen has been removed.

How to Customize your Home screen
Change info at the top

"At A Glance" information is located at the top of your main Home screen. For example, you can learn more about:

Date

1) The weather daily
2) What's next on your schedule?

3) Package delivery reminders from Nest

To modify the information displayed:

1) Touch and hold that area.
2) Select Customize, then Settings.

Change an app

A row of preferred apps will appear at the bottom of your screen.

Uninstall a favorite app: Hold down the app you wish to remove from your favorites. Drag it to a new location on the screen.

Add a favorite app: From the bottom of your screen, swipe up. Maintain your finger on an app. Place the app in a vacant spot among your favorites.

How to Find & delete files on a Google Pixel phone

Your downloaded files are normally found in the Files app on your phone.

Find & open files on a Pixel phone

1) On your mobile, launch the Files app.
2) A list of your file categories will appear.
3) Select a file type, then select More, and finally, You can sort by size, date, or name.

4) To open a file, tap on it.

Delete files

1) On your device, launch the Files app.
2) Select a category, then a file.
3) Then select Delete. 1 file should be moved to the Trash.

Send files from your Pixel phone.

1) Hold the file in your hand.
2) Select Share.
3) Perform additional activities, such as printing or adding to Google Drive.
4) Tap a file to open it.
5) Look for alternatives. If necessary, select More.

How to Transfer Data From An Android Phone To A Pixel

Pair your new Pixel phone with your Android phone to begin data transfers wirelessly.

Step 1: Prepare both phones for setup.

It is required that you have a Google Account. You will be unable to download apps and some files will not be copied to your new Pixel phone if you do not do so.

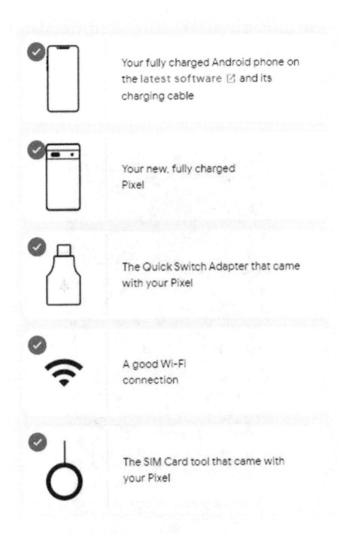

Your fully charged Android phone on the latest software ⬀ and its charging cable

Your new, fully charged Pixel

The Quick Switch Adapter that came with your Pixel

A good Wi-Fi connection

The SIM Card tool that came with your Pixel

To begin, make sure you have:

1) Your fully charged current Android phone with the most recent software.
2) Fully charged, your new Pixel phone.
3) A steady Wi-Fi connection.

4) To use a physical SIM card with your new Pixel, you'll need your SIM card and a SIM card insertion tool.

Step 2: connect your phones.

1) Switch on both your new Pixel phone and your old Android phone.

2) Select a Pixel or Android device on your brand-new Pixel phone.
3) Select Set up from the notification on your current Android phone. There will be a QR code reader visible.
4) Alternatively, you can manually use your Camera app to scan the QR code.
5) Using your old Android phone, scan the QR code on your new Pixel phone.
6) Your new Pixel phone inherits the active Wi-Fi connection from your old Android phone. Connect your Android phone to a Wi-Fi network right away if it isn't already connected.

Step 3: Prepare your Pixel phone.

1) Put in the SIM card. If offered, you can also get an eSIM from your service provider. Just follow the instructions on the screen to start the download.

2) In your Pixel phone, insert your SIM or eSIM card. Follow the instructions on the screen to transfer.

3) Enter the screen lock from your current Android phone on your Pixel handset.
4) Your Pixel phone and Google Accounts are now synchronized.
5) It's possible to configure fingerprint and face unlock.

Step 4: Back up the apps and data.

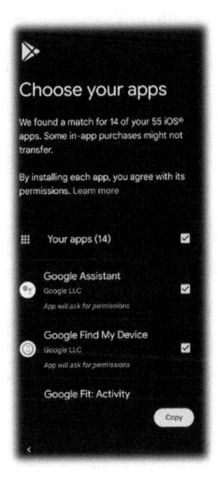

Choose the data to be copied from your current Android device. Data that can be transmitted includes apps, Google Accounts, and SMS messages.

How to Transfer data from a cloud backup

Perform the following actions:

1) Begin the setup process by pressing the Start button.
2) Connect to the internet via Wi-Fi or your cell carrier.
3) When prompted to "Copy Apps & Data," select Next.
4) When prompted to "Use your old device," select Cannot use the old phone.
5) To access your backup, sign into your Google Account and follow the on-screen directions.

Copy data from your old phone with a cable

Perform the following actions:

1) Start by pressing the Start button.
2) Sign up for a Wi-Fi network or a mobile carrier.
3) When prompted to "Copy Apps & Data," choose Next and then Make a copy of your data.
4) When prompted to "Use your old device," select Next.

5) Turn your Android device on and unlock it.
6) Connect one end of your charging wire to your Android device.
7) First, connect the Quick Switch Adapter to your Pixel phone, then the other end of the cable to your Pixel phone.
8) What happens if you are unable to access a cable? A portion of your data can be transferred wirelessly.
9) Select Trust on your Android device.
10)   Your data is listed on your Pixel phone.
11) Choose Copy if you want to copy all of your data.
12)   To replicate only a portion of the data, disable anything you don't want to duplicate.
13)   Select the Copy.
14)   You can use your phone after your transfer is finished.
15)   Utilizing WiFi, copy data

Perform the following actions on your Pixel phone:

1) Hit the Start menu.
2) Make a connection to a mobile provider or Wi-Fi network.
3) When asked to "Copy Apps & Data," select Copy your data by touching Next.
4) To "Use your old device," click the prompt and choose Next.

5) If asked to "Find your old phone's cable," choose "No cable."

6) In the notification, tap OK.

7) Activate and unlock your present mobile device.

8) Open the notification on your old phone to set up your new one.

9) You will see a list of your data on your Pixel phone.

10) Choose Copy if you want to copy all of your data.

11) To replicate only a portion of the data, disable anything you don't want to duplicate.

12) Select the Copy.

13) You are free to use your phone after the transfer is finished.

14) It might take a while for your apps to load after you move your data.

How to Transfer data from an iPhone to a Pixel

Step 1: Prepare to charge both of your phones

Step 2: Determine what you require.

Your fully charged iPhone device on the latest software ☑

The charging cable from your former iPhone device

Your new, fully charged Pixel

The Quick Switch Adapter that came with your Pixel

A good Wi-Fi connection

The SIM Card tool that came with your Pixel

Find what you require.

1) An iPhone-compatible cable, like the one you use to charge it

2) Your SIM card and SIM card insertion tool, unless you have an eSIM

Step 3: On your iPhone

Disable iMessage and Facetime.

If your iPhone is managed by an organization, such as a corporation or a school, it may be limited in its transfer.

Step 4: On your Pixel

1) Start your Pixel by pressing the Get Started button. On your phone, you can change the language or vision settings.

Step 5: Configure another device iOS

Select iPhone or iPad.

Step 6: To access your Google account, make sure you're connected to a Wi-Fi or mobile network.

1) If you are unable to connect to your mobile network, insert a SIM card to connect to a Wi-Fi network.
2) Open your Google Account and log in.

3) Please remember that a Google Account is required. If not, you won't be able to download apps and some content won't transfer over to your replacement smartphone.
4) Get your eSIM and connect to a mobile network. Otherwise, place your SIM card in as directed.

Step 7: Configure how you want to unlock your device

1) Configure Fingerprint Unlock
2) Configure Face Unlock

Step 8: Connect the phones and transfer your data.

1) On your Pixel phone, press the Start button.
2) Sign up for a Wi-Fi network or a mobile carrier.
3) When prompted to "Copy data from your iPhone or iPad," press the Next button. Make a copy of your data.
4) When prompted to "Use your old device," select Next.
5) Switch on and unlock your iPhone.
6) Slide the iPhone charging cord's one end into the device.
7) First, connect the Quick Switch Adapter to your Pixel phone, then the other end of the cable to your Pixel phone.

8) What happens if you are unable to access a cable? Although cable can transfer a greater variety of data types, it is preferred when exchanging certain types of data wirelessly.

9) On your iPhone, tap Trust.

10) A list of your data types shows up on your Pixel phone.

11) It should be noted that the amount of iPhone storage may occasionally generate a capacity warning since it comprises system files or linked iCloud data. Ignore the warning and proceed if you are satisfied that all of the data on the device can be transferred. Using an iPhone Go to Settings, General, then iPhone Storage to view how much on-device storage is being used.

12) To copy all of your information, select Copy.

13) To copy only a portion of the data, uncheck the boxes next to the items you don't want to copy.

14) Choose Copy.

15) While your Pixel is being transferred, you can continue configuring it.

16) Once the transfer is finished, review the transfer summary screens to see the findings and recommendations for transferring any missing content.

How to Find, open, and Close apps on a Pixel phone

Some apps will appear on your Home screens, while others will appear in All Apps. You can open apps, switch between apps, and search for two apps at the same time.

Find & open apps

From anywhere

1) Swipe from the bottom to the top of your screen.
2) Tap the app you wish to launch.

From shortcuts

1) Hold your finger on the app.
2) Choose one of your alternatives.

From your Home Screen

1) Use your screen's bottom swipe to swipe upward.
2) Type the app's name into the Search bar to open it.

How to Change Between Recent Apps

1) Lift from the bottom, hold, and then let go.
2) Select Recent applications if you're using Android Go's three-button navigation.

3) To access the desired app, swipe to the left or right.
4) To open the desired app, tap it.

Close the apps

Close one application: From the bottom, swipe upward; then, hold and let go. On the app, swipe up.

Shut down every application: From the bottom, swipe upward; then, hold and let go. Make a left-to-right swipe. Go to the left and choose Clear All.

1) To close every app on Android Go, swipe up from the bottom of the screen, hold it, and then release it. Click on Clear all at the bottom.

Find the Home screen: Navigate to the home screen.

Stop background apps from running:

1) Swipe down twice from the top of the screen to access Quick Settings.
2) Try the following to find out how many apps are open and running in the background:
3) Click the #active apps button in the lower-left corner.
4) Alternatively, tap the number next to Settings and Power at the bottom right.

5) To stop using the current app, tap Stop.
6) You won't run out of battery life or memory if you don't close apps. Android takes care of these automatically.

How to Get New Apps

More apps can be found in the Play Store app.

How to Install apps on your Pixel phone.

You may download both free and paid apps from Google Play on your Android phone.

Install applications from Google Play.

1) Open Google Play.
2) Use the Google Play Store app on your device.
3) On your PC, navigate to play.google.com.
4) Look for the app you want.
5) To confirm the app's dependability, look into what others are saying about it.
6) Under the app's title, look at the star ratings and number of downloads.
7) Individual reviews can be found by scrolling down to the "Ratings and Reviews" section.
8) After selecting an app, press Install (for free apps) or the app's cost.

Get apps from other websites.

Important: Downloading apps from unknown sources may jeopardize the security of your phone and personal information.

1) Your phone could be damaged or lose data.
2) Your private information may have been compromised or hacked.

Download apps from other sources.

Begin downloading the application from a different location.

1) Follow the on-screen directions. You may need to select Ok, then Install, depending on the source.
2) On the notification that shows, tap Settings.
3) Allow from this source should be set to true.

Disable getting apps from other sources.

1) Launch the Settings app on your phone.
2) Select Special app access, then Apps, and finally Install Unknown Apps.
3) Press the application that no longer asks you to install unidentified apps.

Allow from this source should be disabled.

1) Assist Google in protecting itself against malicious apps from other sources.

2) If you install apps from sources other than Google Play, your phone may submit app information to Google.
3) This information helps Google protect everyone from dangerous applications. Log information, app-related URLs, device ID, Android version, and IP address may be included in the data.

How to Change Your App Settings

Set or clear default apps

If you have multiple apps that do the same job, you can choose which one to run by default.

Set default apps on your phone

Pick when asked

1) When prompted by your phone, open the selected app.
2) Decide if you want to use that app once or frequently for this task.
3) Your smartphone won't ask you again which app to use for that task if you select Always.
4) Clear the default to make your device ask again.

Choose at any time

1) Go into the Settings app on your device.
2) Select Default Apps by tapping on Apps.

3) Tapping it will allow you to modify the default.
4) Choose the app that you wish to set as your default.

Clear an app's default settings from your phone.

1) Go into the Settings app on your device.
2) Select app
3) Pick the app you want to be the exception rather than the default. First, select See all apps or App info if it's not visible.
4) By default, tap the Open button.

Disable Navigate to a supported link.

After clearing the default, your device will prompt you to select an app the next time you make that operation.

How to change the app permissions.

Some apps, such as your camera or contacts list, can be granted access to your device's functions. A notification will be sent to you by an app requesting permission to access certain functions on your smartphone, which you can approve or deny. You may also change permissions for an individual app or by permission type in your device's settings.

Change the app's permissions.

1) Open the Settings app.
2) Select app
3) Select the app that you wish to modify. If it's not visible, choose View All Apps. Select your app next.
4) Choose Permissions.
5) Any app permissions you granted or denied will be noted here.
6) To modify a permission setting, tap it and select Allow or Don't Allow.

For location, camera, and microphone permissions, you may be able to select the following options:

Every time: The app can utilize the permission at any moment, even while you are not using it.

Allow only when using the app: The permission can only be used by the app while you are using it.

Ask every time: Each time you launch the app, permission will be sought. It can continue to use the privilege until you uninstall the program.

Allow: Even if you use the permission, the app cannot use it.

Change permissions according to their type.

It is possible to examine which apps have the same rights. You can see which apps have access to your calendar, for example.

1) Open the Settings app.
2) Select Security & Privacy, then Privacy, and then Permissions.
3) Choose a permission type.
4) Any apps that you gave or denied permission to will be mentioned here.
5) To change an app's permissions, tap it and then pick your permission settings.

Remove permissions for unused apps automatically.

1) Open the Settings app.
2) Select app
3) Select the app that you wish to modify.
4) Press If it's not there, browse through all of the apps. Select your app next.
5) In the "Unused app settings," select the option to "Pause app activity if not in use."

How to Sync your apps with your Google Account

You can adjust how your apps sync messages, emails, and other recent data in your Google Account.

Turn off auto-sync.

1) Open your device's Settings app.
2) Passwords and accounts should be selected.
3) If your phone has multiple accounts, choose which one you wish to sync.
4) Select Account sync.
5) Turn off any apps that you don't wish to sync automatically.
6) Removing an app does not mean turning off its auto-sync feature. All it does is stop the app from updating your data on its own.

Sync your account manually

1) Launch the Settings application.
2) Select About, followed by Google Account, and then Account Sync.
3) If your device has multiple accounts, choose which one you wish to sync.
4) Click on More, and then select Sync Now.
5) All Google apps, even those without auto-sync, update your account information when you use manual sync.

How to Delete, disable & manage unused apps

Delete apps on Google Play

Delete apps that you installed

1) Navigate to the Google Play Store app.
2) In the upper right corner, tap the Profile symbol.
3) Tap Manage applications & devices, then Manage.
4) Select the name of the app you want to remove.
5) Select Uninstall.

Disable apps that came with your phone

Some pre-installed system apps on your Pixel phone cannot be removed. Most system apps, on the other hand, can be disabled.

1) Open the Settings app
2) Tap Apps, then All Apps, and finally the app you want to deactivate.
3) Tap Disable at the top.

How to Manage Unused Apps

If you haven't used an app in a long time, Android will optimize it by:

1) To clear up space, delete temporary files.
2) Restrict app permissions.
3) Stop running useless programs in the background.

Stop notifications from being sent by unused apps.

1) Go to Apps and then underused apps to review underused and optimized apps.
2) Go to App Info and then Unused Apps to exclude any individual program from this feature. Then, deactivate the Pause app activity if not in use.

How to Make & receive phone calls

Phone calls can be placed using the Phone app as well as other apps or widgets that display your contacts.

In most cases, you can call a phone number by simply tapping it wherever you see it. You may be able to copy phone numbers on Google Chrome by hitting underlined numbers.

Make a phone call.

To use the phone app, you must first accept the option to make it your default.

Launch the Phone app on your phone.

Choose who to call:

1) To enter a phone number, tap Dialpad.
2) Select a saved contact by tapping Contacts. We may propose contacts to call based on your call history.
3) Tap Recents to select numbers you've recently phoned.
4) Tap Favorites to access contacts saved in Favorites.

5) Select Call.

6) Click the "End call" button once the call is over. Drag the minimized call bubble to the lower-right corner of the screen.

How to Accept or decline a phone call

Upon receiving a call, the caller's number, contact name, or caller ID details are shown on the screen. Google overlays the word Verified over the caller's name or number when it can validate a phone number.

1) When your phone is locked, swipe the white circle across the top of the screen or hit the Answer button to take a call.

2) If your phone is locked, swipe the white circle to the bottom of the screen or select Dismiss to end the call. If their call is declined, callers can leave a message.

3) Swipe up from the Message icon New message to reject the call and text the caller.

Tips: Your current call is put on hold when you answer one while on another.

If Google Assistant is enabled, you can answer or decline calls with your voice. Saying something like, "Hey Google, answer the call,"

How to Make use of phone call options.

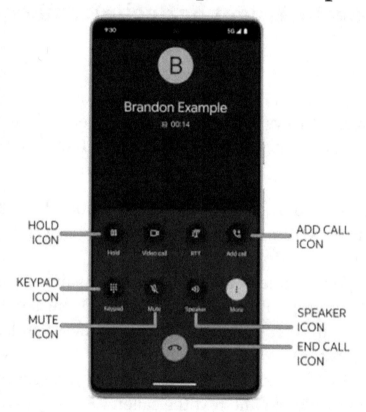

While a call is in progress:

1) Tap Dialpad to display the keypad.

2) To switch between the speakerphone, earpiece, and any connected Bluetooth headsets, tap the Speaker.
3) Tap Mute to mute or unmute your microphone.
4) Press Hold to halt a discussion without cutting it off. To take the call, tap Hold again.
5) Access to this feature will be available to customers who enroll in the catch phone service. If not, the screen will display an error message.
6) Tap Switch to move between the open calls.
7) Select Call merge to group all active calls into a single conference call.
8) Select the Home screen to reduce the call.
9) Drag the call bubble to move it.
10) Drag the call bubble to the "Hide" button located at the bottom of the screen to make it disappear.

To: using a few devices and carriers

Make a video call instead: Select a video call. video conference.

Transferring a call that is in progress to a different number

1) Select Add Call while on an ongoing call.
2) Provide a phone number.
3) Select Call.

4) After the call is connected, tap Transfer. The phone number you entered will receive your call.

How to make phone calls using Wi-Fi.

Before you may make Wi-Fi calls, you must enable the option in your settings.

Enable Wi-Fi calling.

Use a mobile carrier's Wi-Fi calling

1) Launch the Phone app.
2) Select More, then Settings.
3) Tap on Calls.
4) Choose Wi-Fi calling. If you do not see this option, your carrier does not support it.

Use Wi-Fi to make a phone call.

1) Once you've enabled Wi-Fi calling, you may make a call just like any other. When you're connected to the internet, you'll see "Internet Call" or "Wi-Fi calling" on the notification screen.
2) If you don't have Wi-Fi, your calls will be routed through your cell carrier, if you have one.

How to View and Delete Call History

A list of calls you've made, answered, or missed is available. You can also remove calls from that list.

See your call history

1) Launch the Phone app on your device.
2) Select Recents.
3) The following icons will appear next to every call in your list:
   a) **Missed calls:** Incoming calls that were missed
   b) **Received calls:** Calls that you took and responded to incoming phone calls
   c) **Outgoing calls**: Calls you placed

View call information

1) Tap the call in your history and choose Call details to get more information about it.
2) Every call made to that number will be listed, along with information about when it occurred, how long it lasted, and whether it was an inbound or outgoing call.

Add phone numbers to your contact list.

Press the phone number and select Add to Contact or Add to Call History to add it to your contacts.

Remove calls from your call history

1) Launch the Phone app on your device.
2) Select Recents.
3) Select a phone number or contact.
4) Select Call Details.
5) Tap Trash Delete at the top.

How to Delete all of your call history.

1) Launch the Phone app on your device.
2) Select Recents.
3) To access Call History, tap More.
4) Select Clear call history after tapping More.
5) When asked to erase your call history, tap OK.

How to check your voicemail

Call your voicemail service to listen to your voicemail. You can view a list of your voicemails in your Phone app on some devices and providers.

Select a message notification.

When you receive a voicemail, you can check it using the notification on your phone.

1) Swipe down from the screen's top.
2) Select Voicemail.

Call the voicemail box.

Call your voicemail service to check your messages.

1) Open the phone app.
2) Tap the Dialpad on the bottom.
3) Touch and hold 1

Change your voicemail settings.

1) Open the phone app.
2) To access additional options, tap More in the upper right corner.
3) Tap Voicemail, then Settings.

You may

1) You can change the carrier that receives your voicemails. Select Advanced Settings and then Service.
2) Set up your voice mailbox as follows: Tap Advanced Settings, followed by Setup.
3) Modify your notification settings as follows: Select Notifications.
4) To enable Vibrate, go to Notifications, then Advanced, and finally Vibration.

How to Use more Phone app features

When you make or receive a call with caller ID and spam protection activated, you may receive information on unknown callers or businesses, as well as warnings about potential spam callers.

How to Use caller ID & spam protection

Your phone may need to send call information to Google to use caller ID and spam protection.

If someone from outside your contact list contacts you or calls you, Google receives their phone number to assist in identifying its business Caller ID name or determining whether the call is spam.

Turn off or enable caller ID and spam protection.

Caller ID and spam filtering are enabled by default. You have the option to disable it.

Your phone may need to send call information to Google to use caller ID and spam protection. It does not control whether your phone number is displayed when you call.

1) On your device, launch the Phone app.

2) Select More options. More is followed by Settings, and lastly the Spam and Call Screen.
3) Activate or deactivate caller and spam ID.
4) **Optional:** To stop spam calls, turn on "Filter spam calls." You will not receive missed calls or voicemail notifications, but filtered calls will appear in your call history, and your voicemail will be available.
5) Google Caller ID shows the names of businesses and services listed on Google My Business. It also looks for directory matches, which provide callers with information about their work or school accounts. On caller ID, a corporate category may appear.
6) To change the name on your work or school account, please contact your administrator.
7) If you want to change your company's name or phone number, you should update your business information.

Turn on the caller ID announcements.

To hear a caller's name or number announced, turn on the Caller ID announcement.

1) On your device, open the Phone app.
2) Select additional options. More, Settings, Caller ID notification, and finally Declare caller ID are the options.

Choose one of the following:

1) Always
2) When wearing a headset

Mark calls as spam

To avoid future calls from that number and report the spammer, mark all calls from that number as spam.

1) On your device, open the Phone app.
2) At the bottom, choose Recent.
3) Select the call you wish to report as spam.
4) Choose between blocking or reporting spam.
5) To report a call as spam, simply touch and hold. Then select either Block or Report Spam.

How to Use the Phone app to record calls

You may use your Phone app to do the following:

1) Calls from unknown numbers should always be recorded.
2) Calls from specific contacts should always be recorded.

You can listen to previously stored recordings. You can also specify the length of time that recorded calls should be retained.

Follow these steps to record your phone calls:

1) On your Android device, launch the Phone app.
2) Select More choices. At the upper right, select More, then Settings, and then Call Recording.
3) Under "Always record," check the box next to Selected numbers.
4) Select the Always record chosen numbers checkbox.
5) Tap Add in the upper right corner.
6) Select a contact.
7) Always record is selected.
8) Repeat these procedures for each contact you want to keep track of.
9) You can also enable call recording by opening a contact. At the bottom right of the contact card, tap Edit contact and select Always Record calls.

Start a recording from a call

To protect the privacy of all users, when you begin recording, you alert both parties with a disclosure that the call is being recorded. When you stop recording, both parties receive notice that the conversation is no longer being recorded.

1) Launch the phone app.
2) Make or receive phone calls.

3) Go to the ongoing call screen and tap Record.
4) Stop recording by tapping. Turn off the recording. Put an end to the recording.
5) Your recordings are kept private because they are saved on your smartphone. Outside of the device, calls are not saved or backed up.

Find a recorded call

Follow these steps to locate your recording.

1) Open the phone app.
2) Choose Recent.
3) Tap on the recorded caller.
4) Go to the "Recents" page and select the player from which you recorded the most recent call.
5) If you've previously recorded a call, choose History. Then choose a recording from the list of calls.
6) Click the Play button.
7) To share a recorded call, select Share.
8) You can send recorded calls to apps that support them, such as email and messaging.

Determine how long to keep recorded calls.

1) Launch the Phone app on your Android device.
2) Select More choices. At the upper right, select More, then Settings, and then Call Recording.

3) Under "Recordings," click the Delete button.
4) Set the duration of a recorded call before it is automatically deleted.
5) Select the Confirm button.
6) To erase all recordings, tap erase all recordings immediately and then Delete.

Delete a previously recorded call

1) Start the Phone app.
2) Choose Recents
3) Find the phone number or contact information for the recorded call you want to delete.
4) Choose History.
5) Swipe left to find the recording in the list of calls.

How to Use Hold for Me

When you call a firm and are placed on hold, you may tell Google Assistant to wait for you and notify you when a support agent is available to speak with you. You can help improve Hold for Me by contributing your audio and transcript after your call.

Turn the setting on or off

1) Start the Phone app.
2) Select more then go to settings.
3) Please hold the button for me.

4) Switch on or off Hold for Me.
5) Select Hold for Me while on the phone.

Turn your phone to vibrate only or silence.

1) Start the Phone app.
2) Contact a business over the phone.
3) Tap Hold for me, then Start after being put on hold.
4) A card with the words "Don't hang up" will appear on the screen while you're on hold.
5) A prompt stating "Someone is waiting to speak with you" will appear when a support professional is available to speak with you.
6) Tap the button to return to the call.

Share information from your call.

It is crucial to understand that once your data is sent, it cannot be reversed.

1) Start the Phone app.
2) At the bottom, select Recent.
3) Under the call log entry, tap Help us improve, then Yes, continue, and then Continue.
4) Fill out the text box if you wish to send feedback.
5) Choose Send.
   - To share your information without disclosing your email address, go to the Send Feedback

screen and select Google user by tapping the Down arrow next to the "From" field.

How to Use Direct My Call

When you call a business with an automated menu, Direct My Call displays on screen what the automated voice says as well as the menu selections available to you via tappable number buttons. You can select a menu choice by tapping the buttons on your screen.

Turn on or off Direct My Call.

1) Launch the Phone app.
2) Tap More and then Settings in the upper right corner.
3) Choose Direct My Call.
4) Direct My Call can be turned on or off.
5) If you want to end Direct My Call while it's still active, touch Close in the top left corner of the screen.

Share data from your call

It is important to remember that the action is finished as soon as your data is sent.

Once your call is over, you can help Direct My Call get better by sharing your audio and transcript.

1) Start the Phone app.
2) At the bottom, select Recent.
3) Click Continue, then Continue, and then Continue to assist us in making this better.
4) It is optional for you to enter feedback in the text box.
5) Click Send in the top right corner.
6) To share your data with Google without disclosing your email address, go to the Send Feedback screen and select Google user by tapping the Down arrow next to the "From" field.

How to Back up & sync device contacts

Some of your phone or tablet's contacts may not have been saved as Google contacts. Certain apps, for instance, store contacts in device storage, making them exclusive to that device. Modifications made to these contacts do not propagate to other Google services or devices that are signed in. These contacts might disappear if the device is ever misplaced or breaks.

Save device contacts as Google contacts to ensure that your contacts are backed up and synchronized with all of your devices. All Google services allow you to access and manage your Google contacts from any connected device. When you sign in, the contacts can be automatically synced to a new device if the original device is lost or destroyed.

Back up and synchronize contact.

Save device contacts as Google contacts for syncing and backup purposes:

1) Open the "Settings" app on your Android tablet or phone.
2) Select Google, followed by Google apps, synchronize device contacts, sync Google Contacts, and automatically sync and backup device contacts.
3) Decide whether to sync and automatically back up device contacts.
4) Decide which account you wish to save your contacts in. Contacts can only be saved to a single Google Account at once.

Remove contacts from your Google Account and cease storing contacts on your device as Google contacts.

To stop device contacts from being automatically saved as Google contacts, follow these steps:

1) Open the "Settings" app on your Android tablet or phone.

2) Select Google, followed by Google apps, synchronize device contacts, sync Google Contacts, and automatically sync and backup device contacts.

Turn off the device's automatic contact synchronization and backup.

Prior Google contacts will remain in your account until they are removed manually.

How to Change Phone App Settings

Modify your call settings

You can adjust the call ringtone, vibration settings, rapid answers, and call history display on your phone.

Modify the sound and vibration settings

1) Launch the Phone app.
2) Select More, then Settings.
3) Sounds and vibrations can be activated by tapping.
4) Tap the Phone ringtone to access the available ringtones.
5) Tap Also vibrate for calls to enable your phone to vibrate when you receive a call.

6) Choose Dial pad tones if you want to hear sounds when you tap the dial pad. (If "Dial pad tones" is not visible, select "Keypad tones.")

Change how callers' names are formatted and listed

1) Launch the Phone app.
2) Select More, then Settings.
3) Select Display options.
4) Tap Sort by to modify the way your phone arranges calls in your call history.
5) Tap Name format to modify the way your phone shows contact names in your history.

Change text responses

If you are unable to answer a phone call, you can instead send an automated text message. Here's how you can change your auto-text messages:

1) Launch the Phone app.
2) Select More, then Settings.
3) Select Quick Replies.
4) Select an option from the list.
5) Edit your response.
6) Tap Ok.

How to Block or unblock a phone number

You can block a phone number if you don't want to receive calls from it. When the number attempts to call you, your phone automatically declines the call.

Block a number

1) Launch the Phone app.
2) Tap More, followed by Call history.

3) Tap an incoming call from the number you want to ban.
4) Block or report spam.

Block unknown numbers

1) Launch the Phone app.
2) More should be selected
3) Select Settings, then Blocked numbers.
4) Unknown should be enabled.

5) This prevents calls from private or unknown numbers. You will continue to receive calls from numbers not in your contacts.

Unblock a phone number

1) Launch the Phone app.
2) More should be selected.
3) Select Settings, then Blocked numbers.
4) Tap Clear and then Unblock next to the number you want to unblock.

How to Take a Pictures

You can take a photo with your phone's camera in a variety of ways. This article will assist you in taking images and locating information for advanced photo settings.

1) Launch the Google Camera application.
2) Point your camera at something and wait for it to focus.

3) Select Capture.

Zoom

Pinch your screen open or closed, double-tap it, or use the bottom slider.

Adjust your camera lens

Take a wider shot with Ultrawide zoom

To catch more individuals and surroundings, use Ultrawide Zoom.

1) Launch the Google Camera app.
2) To zoom out on your screen, pinch it.
3) With auto-focus, you can adjust the subject's sharpness.
4) Point your camera at the subject of your photograph to concentrate on it.
5) Tap on the topic. A white circle appears and moves along with the thing on the screen.
6) Tap Lock to lock the focus and exposure on a moving subject.

Choose how to take a photo

Using your hand

1) Start the Google Camera app.
2) Wait for your camera to focus and absorb light after pointing it towards something.
3) Select Capture.

Using your voice

1) Ask "OK Google, take a picture," instead of "OK Google, take a selfie."
2) **Optional:** Tell the camera to wait 3 to 30 seconds before snapping the photo. For example, "OK Google," "take a picture in 12 seconds."

3) Your Camera app will launch and take a photograph.

With Wear OS

Connect your watch to your phone.

1) Launch the Google Camera app.
2) To access the Remote card, swipe up from the bottom of the screen on your watch.
3) To take a photo, press the shutter button on your watch.
4) Your watch will begin to vibrate and flash.
5) You'll see a thumbnail of the photo on your watch.

How to Use your phone to take a selfie.

You can snap a self-portrait (selfie) with your Pixel device's front camera.

Flip your lens

1) Launch the Google Camera application.
2) To use your front camera, tap Switch.
3) Choose Capture.
4) To take a selfie without pressing buttons, flip your lens.
5) Rotate your phone so that it faces you first, then back toward you.
6) Rep step 1 to turn your lens again.

Choose how to save selfies.

Selfies can be saved either mirrored or unmirrored. If you save a previously seen selfie, it will not appear inverted when you take another selfie.

1) To mirror or not mirror your selfies, tap the Down arrow at the top of your camera, then Settings.

Change the look of a selfie

How to Retouch a Selfie

Selfies and Portrait mode images can have their faces edited.

1) Tap the Down arrow to edit a selfie or a picture taken in portrait mode.
2) Under "Face Retouching":
3) Tap Smooth or Subtle.

Tip: The results of face editing are only visible in the final image.

Brighten a selfie

To brighten selfies, switch to the front camera first. To brighten selfies, tap the Down arrow and select Selfie Illumination.

Get a selfie to help with verbal cues

Guided Frame notifies you when you're in position for a selfie. Your face is surrounded by a dotted frame, and voice signals and vibrations indicate when the photo should be taken.

Turn on TalkBack to obtain Guided Frame.

1) Open the Settings app on your device.
2) Tap TalkBack, then Accessibility.
3) Turn it on or off Use TalkBack.
4) To use Guided Frame, launch the Google Camera app:
5) Keep the front camera button pressed.
6) Double-tap the front camera button to activate Selfie mode.
7) Take note of any auditory instructions or vibrations.
8) The Camera app captures your selfie.

How to Use Top Shots to Capture Motion Shots

Capture something in motion with motion photos, and then utilize Top Shot to choose a favorite shot from your motion photo or film.

Take an action pan or long exposure photo with Motion Mode.

1) Start the Google Camera app.

2) Scroll down to Motion.
3) Choose the blur effect that you want to use:
   a) **Action Pan:** Apply a playful background blur using Action Pan. To get a unique blur in the background, hold the camera steady or track a moving subject. Once you are satisfied with the picture, press the Capture button.
   b) **Long exposure:** This technique works well for giving a moving subject a creative blur. You can either follow a moving subject or keep your camera motionless to achieve an artistic blur. Once you're satisfied with the picture, press the Capture button.

Save specific shots from a motion photo or movie with Top Shot.

When you take a photo or record a short video, you may receive suggestions for a higher-quality Top Shot.

Switch on Top Shot.

1) Start your device's Camera app.
2) In the lower-left corner, tap Settings.
3) Top Shot should be turned on or off.
4) Select a Top Shot

5) Use Top Shot to select your best motion photo or film shot after taking motion picture footage of something in motion.
6) Store suggested photos with HDR and at a higher resolution.
7) Select More, Export, Video, and then Export to save the motion picture as a video.

Turn on or off Frequent Faces.

You can help the camera on your Pixel, recognize and recommend better photographs of the faces you most frequently snap or film.

Your camera knows which shots feature the faces you typically capture and suggests them to you when it discovers and suggests other images or short films within your own. Then, the camera suggests enhanced versions of those faces.

When you enable Frequent Faces, your camera remembers which faces it photos or captures. Instead of being sent to Google, all facial data is stored on your device. Your data is destroyed when you disable Frequent Faces.

To activate Frequent Faces, follow these steps:

1) Start the Google Camera app.

2) Tap Settings and select more in the bottom left corner.
3) Select Frequent Faces.
4) Enable Frequent Faces.

How to take photos in low light or at night

If your device is steady, you can snap photographs in low light or of the night sky without using the flash.

Use Night Sight to take images in low light.

1) Start the Google Camera app.
2) Choose Night Sight from the carousel of photo modes.
3) Select Capture.
4) While your device takes the picture, hold your breath for a short while.
5) When you capture a shot in low-light situations when your camera is in Default or Portrait mode, Night Sight activates automatically.

How to turn off Automatic Night Sight for a single shot

1) Tap Night Sight on the right.
2) Slide the slider from Max to Off to make modifications.
3) Select Settings.
4) Change the More Light setting to None.

How to take a panorama

1) Start the Google Camera app.
2) In the photo mode carousel, select Panorama.
3) Select Capture.

4) While moving the camera horizontally, keep the lens steady. Maintain the white frame's alignment.
5) Rotate your phone vertically to capture a vertical panorama. Then, pan your camera up and down.
6) When you're through taking pictures, tap Stop recording.
7) To cancel a photo, press Close

Take a 360-degree photosphere

You may use your Pixel camera to make various sorts of 360-degree picture spheres, such as panorama photo spheres and fisheye photos. To make a 360-degree photosphere, follow these steps:

1) Launch the Google Camera app.
2) On the photo mode carousel, tap Photo Sphere and then Capture.

1) The target circle should be positioned above a white dot. The dot will become blue before disappearing.
2) Proceed to the next white dot with the camera, maintaining a steady lens.

3) Repeat until no more white dots appear, or tap Done

To alter the type of your Photo Sphere, follow these steps:

1) Tap Settings in the lower left corner.
2) Tap the Panorama photosphere to capture a 360-degree image.
3) Tap Horizontal to take a horizontal picture.
4) Tap Vertical to take a vertical picture.

5) To capture an image with a wide arc, tap broad-angle.
6) Tap Fisheye to take a fisheye picture.

How to Use Macro Focus to get a close-up.

Macro Focus can be used to capture microscopic details in your images and movies, such as flower petals or dew drops.

Macro Focus should be used as follows:

1) Launch the Google Camera app.
2) Bring your device up near the topic.
3) To bring the focus back to the screen, tap it.
4) Take a snapshot or video of the Macro bloom as it appears.

Tips:

1) Steer clear of obstructing the light source or shading your subject.
2) Press to make Macro Focus active or inactive.
3) Tap the area of the screen that you want to concentrate on to narrow down your topic.

How to take a photo or video from a distance

Take distant pictures of your subjects. Certain Pixel devices have 30x zoom thanks to the newest zoom lens technology. When zoomed to 15x, zoom stabilization is activated by default.

1) Start the Google Camera application.
2) Get closer to your topic.
3) To make fast adjustments, press the 2x or 5x zoom button located above the shutter.
4) To reveal the zoom slider and improve accuracy, pinch the screen or swipe across the zoom buttons.
5) Tap your subject to focus.
6) Take a picture.

How to take a video

On your phone, you may record in both real-time and slow motion. You can also capture time-lapse videos that accelerate when played back.

Create a video.

1) To record a video, open the Google Camera app and tap and hold the Capture button.
2) Open the Google Camera application.
3) If in Photo mode, switch to Video mode. Switch to video mode.
4) To start recording, tap Record.
5) Pause your video to add breaks. To resume recording, tap Record.

6) To take a high-resolution snapshot while recording a video, select Capture.
7) To stop recording, press the Stop button.

Make use of video effects.

Make a video smoother

1) Launch the Google Camera app.
2) If in Photo mode, switch to Video mode. Switch to video mode.
3) Select Stabilization from the Video Settings menu in the lower-left corner.
4) Choose the type of stabilization you want.
5) To record light movements, select Standard.
6) To take still photos, tap Locked.
7) Tap Active to capture fast movement.
8) You can select the level of stability for each mode.

Get cinematic video effects.

When recording in Cinematic mode, you can blur the background while maintaining focus on your subject. To enable cinematic mode, follow these steps:

1) Open the Google Camera app on your smartphone.
2) If in Camera mode, switch to Video mode. Switch to video mode.

3) Use the swipe gesture to activate Cinematic Blur mode.
4) Press the shutter button to begin recording.
5) Direct your focus by tapping on the subject.

Get vibrant video colors.

When you record HDR video, you get stunning visual colors. Follow these steps to enable 10-bit HDR video:

1) Open the Google Camera application.
2) If in Photo mode, switch to Video mode. Switch to video mode.
3) In the lower-left corner, select Video Settings.

Create a high-quality video.

You can record in 4K at up to 60 frames per second with any of your phone's cameras. Follow the steps below to enable high-resolution video:

1) Launch the Google Camera app.
2) In Camera mode, switch to Video mode. Switch to video mode.
3) In the lower-left corner, select Video Settings.
4) Select 4K under "Resolution."
5) Change the frame rate to 60 frames per second under "Frames/Sec".

How to Make a Slow Motion Video.

Follow these instructions to create a slow-motion video:

1) Start the Google Camera app.
2) If you're in Photo mode, change to Video mode.
3) Slow down the video.
4) To begin recording, tap Record.

5) Tap Capture to take a high-resolution snapshot while simultaneously recording a slow-motion video.

6) To stop recording, use the Stop button.

7) If you want to record exceedingly quick speeds in slow motion, go with 1/8x.

How to Make a time-lapse video.

To capture slow changes over time, such as a sunset:

1) Start the Google Camera app.

2) If you're in Photo mode, change to Video mode. Change to video mode.

3) Switch to Time Lapse mode.

Select how much you want to speed up time. As an illustration:

1) Tap 5 times in 50 seconds to capture 10 seconds of video.
2) Tap 120 times in real life for 20 minutes to capture 10 seconds in a video.
3) Press the Record button.
4) Use Capture to take a high-resolution photo and time-lapse video simultaneously.
5) To stop recording, press the Stop button.

How to Take Motion Photos and Use Top Shot

Use motion photos to capture action, and then use Top Shot to select your best motion photo or film shot.

Use Motion Mode to take an Action Pan or Long Exposure photo

1) Start the Google Camera app.
2) Scroll down to Motion.
3) Choose the blur effect that you want to use:
    a) **Action Pan:** Apply a playful background blur using Action Pan. To get a unique blur in the background, hold the camera steady or

track a moving subject. Once you are satisfied with the picture, press the Capture button.

b) **Long exposure**: This technique works well for giving a moving subject a creative blur. You can either follow a moving subject or keep your camera motionless to achieve an artistic blur. Once you're satisfied with the picture, press the Capture button.

Save specific shots from a motion photo or movie with Top Shot.

When you take a photo or record a short video, you may receive suggestions for a higher-quality Top Shot.

Switch on Top Shot.

1) Start your device's Camera app.
2) In the lower-left corner, tap Settings.
3) Top Shot should be turned on or off.
4) Select a Top Shot
5) Use Top Shot to select your best motion photo or film shot after taking motion picture footage of something in motion.
6) Store suggested photos with HDR and at a higher resolution.
7) Select More, Export, Video, and then Export to save the motion picture as a video.

How to enable Frequent Faces

You can help the camera on your Pixel, recognize and recommend better photographs of the faces you most frequently snap or film. Your camera knows which shots feature the faces you typically capture and suggests them to you when it discovers and suggests other images or short films within your own. Then, better versions of those faces are suggested by the camera. When you enable Frequent Faces, your camera remembers which faces it photos or captures. Instead of being sent to Google, all facial data is stored on your device. Your data is destroyed when you disable Frequent Faces.

To enable Frequent Faces:

1) Launch the Google Camera app.
2) Tap Settings and select more in the bottom left corner.
3) Select Frequent Faces.
4) Enable Frequent Faces.

How to Manage Google Camera

You can delete, save, or find a photo or video using Google Photos

How to Delete photos & videos

1) Open the Google Photos app on your Android phone
2) Access your Google Account.
3) To delete a picture or video, tap and hold it. You have the option of selecting multiple items.
4) Tap Trash Delete at the top.

How to Download your photos or videos

1) Open the Google Photos app
2) Choose a picture or a video.
3) Select More and then Download.

How to Locate your photographs and videos

When you enable backup, your photos are saved to photos.google.com. To locate your photos, take these steps:

1) Open the Google Photos application.
2) Select Pictures.

How to Edit a photo or video on your phone

You can edit or change the appearance of a photo on your Pixel device.

How to Change Your Image Format (RAW + JPEG)

Your camera saves your picture files in JPEG + RAW format when you enable RAW/JPEG in the camera settings. By locating the RAW emblem at the top of your photos, you can tell the difference between RAW and JPEG images.

To allow RAW + JPEG files, take the following actions:

1) Launch the Google Camera app.
2) Tap Settings and select more in the bottom left corner.
3) Under "General options," select Advanced.

Enable RAW/JPEG control.

To enable RAW:

1) In photo mode, tap Settings at the bottom left.
2) Enable RAW + JPEG.

To locate, examine, and modify a RAW file, follow these steps:

1) Launch the Google Photos app.
2) When the RAW + JPEG photo pairs were taken with the RAW mode enabled, the gallery grid will display a "RAW" flag.

3) To view RAW photos, tap.

4) While the JPEG image is visible, tapping on the second tile will reveal the RAW image.

5) To alter RAW, tap Modify.

6) When editing RAW files in your preferred editor, you can choose a default RAW editor straight from Google Photos.

7) Google Photos will automatically back up your RAW images if you enable backup.

Use these steps to work with RAW files:

1) Take a picture in default mode or Night Sight.

2) Select the Home screen.

3) Using gestures, swipe upward from the bottom of the screen to navigate.

4) To use the two- or three-button navigation, tap Home.

5) Start using Google Photos.

6) Select Raw in the lower right corner after selecting Library.

How to Straighten, adjust, or crop a photo
Use gridlines to straighten photos

1) Launch the Google Camera app.

2) Tap Settings in the lower left corner.

3) Tap select more, followed by Grid type.

4) Choose the grid type you desire.

Adjust the photo's ratio

1) Launch the Google Camera app.
2) Tap Settings in the lower left corner.

Choose a ratio option:

1) Wide crop (16:9)

2) Full image (4:3)

Crop a photo

Navigate to the photo you wish to modify in the Photos app.

Select Edit photo, then Crop.

Make the borders the size you want.

How to Change the color, light, or photo blur

From the Photos app, select:

1) Locate the photo you wish to modify.
2) Select Edit, then Tools.
3) Here, you can alter a photo's brightness, hue, or blur.

Photo unblur

Photo Unblur can help you fix your blurry photos.

1) Launch your Photos app.
2) Choose the photo to be edited.
3) Tap Edit photo, then Tools, and finally Unblur.

Photo Unblur works with both new and old photographs in your photo collection.

Pop

1) Tap Edit photo, then Tools, and then Pop to open your Photos app.
2) Then, move the scale slider to the desired position.

Color pop

1) In your Photos app, select Edit Photo and then Color Pop.
2) Next, make the right movement with the color pop slider.

Portrait light

You can modify the lighting in your people images with portrait light in your photo editor. Portrait lighting is only accessible when there are four or fewer people in the shot from the waist up.

1) Tap Edit Photo, then Tools, and finally Portrait Light in your Photos app.
2) Place the white ring in the area where you want additional light.
3) Manually or automatically adjust the brightness:
4) Adjust the brightness slider to your liking.
5) • To allow your device to manage the lighting, tap Auto.
6) • Older photos in your Google Photos storage, including ones from different devices, are compatible with Portrait Light. To utilize Portrait light on older photographs, open them in the photographs app.

Adjust brightness or shadows

Adjust the brightness by dragging the Brightness slider to the right.

Adjust shadows: Shadows can be adjusted by adjusting the slider on the right.

How to Use Magic Eraser to erase or minimize distractions

In the Photos app, go to the photo you want to change.

Select Edit, then Tools, and then Magic Eraser.

Choose an idea. You can also use the circle or brush to eliminate unwanted elements from the image.

UNDO   REDO

RESET

Tap Camouflage and blend everything into the photo with the brush.

Finally, press the Done button.

How to Use Magic Editor to reimagine your photos

A photo's elements can be changed or removed, and special-effect presets can be used.

To utilize Magic Editor, go through the following steps:

1) Start the Photos app.
2) Tap the picture you wish to edit.

3) Select Magic Editor by tapping Edit.
4) To use Magic Editor's preset effects, adhere to these instructions:
5) Choose Preset Edit Fix Auto while in Magic Editor mode.
6) Swipe left to browse your selections.
7) Choose a preset.
8) Select the checkbox.
9) Repeat steps 1-3 if you wish to continue editing your shot.
10)   When you're through editing, tap Save Copy.

Move, erase, or resize part of your photo in Magic Editor

Select a portion of your shot using a brush, tap, or draw a circle around it while in Magic Editor mode.

1) Zoom in for additional details.
2) Long press your pick and drag it to the desired spot.
3) To resize your selection, long press it and pinch it with two fingers.
4) Tap Erase to remove your choices.
5) Tap the Checkmark Done to apply the change.
6) Repeat steps 1-2 if you wish to continue editing your shot.
7) When you're through editing, tap Save Copy.

How to Modify the Google Camera app's settings.

You may, for example, toggle location stamps on and off, minimize storage space, and manage dirty lens warnings.

How to Disable the shutter sound.

1) Launch the Google Camera application.
2) Tap Settings and then select more in the bottom left corner.
3) Turn off the camera's audio.

How to Turn off the location stamps in photos and videos.

1) Launch the Google Camera application.
2) Tap Settings and then select more in the bottom left corner.
3) Disable Save location.
4) To view a timestamp for any photo, tap the photo and select More in the bottom right corner. You'll obtain the photo location if you leave location stamps on.

How to Reduce the resolution to conserve storage space.

Photos

1) Launch the Google Camera application.

2) Tap Settings in the lower left corner.

3) Under "Photo," select Full resolution or Medium resolution (which takes up less storage).

Videos

1) Launch the Google Camera application.
2) Change to Video mode.
3) Tap Settings in the lower left corner.
4) Next to "Resolution," choose Full HD.

How to Examine the size of your photo and video storage.

To discover how much storage your Pixel phone has for pictures and videos.

1) Launch the Camera app.
2) Tap Settings, then choose More, and lastly Device Storage from the bottom left menu. At the top of your screen is a display of the storage space you have available.
3) **Take the following actions to boost storage space:** Activate the Storage Saver.
4) **Follow these steps to delete files:** Tap delete.

Turn off the dirty lens warnings.

Your camera may display a warning message if it detects that the lens is dirty. Follow these steps to disable these notifications:

1) Launch the Camera app
2) From the bottom left, select Settings, followed by More, and then Advanced.
3) Disable the "Show Dirty Lens" alert.

Change the way your volume controls work.

1) Launch the Google Camera software.
2) Tap Settings in the lower left corner, then choose More.
3) Press the Volume key after making a gesture.
4) Make a choice.

Activate the flashlight.

To enable flash for brighter photos, follow these steps:

1) Launch the Camera app
2) Select Settings from the bottom left corner, then Flash.

How To Keep Your Private Photographs And Videos Hidden.

The Google Photo app allows you to save sensitive photographs and videos to a folder that is protected by your device's screen lock. Items in the Locked Folder are not visible in the picture grid, memories, search, or albums, and they are inaccessible to other smartphone apps that use your images and videos.

Create a locked folder.

1) Launch the Google Photos app.
2) Go to Library, then Utilities, and finally Locked Folder.
3) Create a locked folder.
4) At this point, you can also enable Backup for Locked Folder.
5) To unlock your device, follow the on-screen prompts. If your folder is empty, it will display "Nothing here yet."
6) To use Locked Folder, your device must have a screen lock installed.
7) The password for your Locked Folder matches the password for your device's screen lock.

Make a backup of your Locked Folder.

You can enable automatic backups for your Locked Folder.

When you enable backup for Locked Folder, you can access it from other devices by logging in using your

Google Account. Backup for Locked Folder can be turned on or off.

1) Open Google Photos on your Android phone.
2) Log in to your Google account.
3) Tap on your profile image or initial in the upper right corner.
4) Tap Photos, then Settings, Backup, and Locked Folder Backup.

Manually back up your locked folder.

Individual photos and videos in your Locked Folder can be manually backed up.

1) Open Google Photos
2) Log in to your Google account.
3) Go to Library, then Utilities, and finally Locked Folder.
4) Use your device's screen lock when requested.
5) Select photos or movies to back up with a long push.
6) At the bottom, choose Back up.

Save images directly from the Pixel camera to the Locked Folder.

1) Start by opening the Google Pixel camera app.
2) In the lower-left corner, select Gallery.
3) Hold your finger on the last image in the gallery.

4) To save your photos, choose Photo Gallery or Locked Folder.
5) Take a photo. Photos taken with Locked Folder enabled are saved to the Locked Folder automatically.
6) Long press the circle to the right of the Shutter to view the most recent photo you took.
7) Select Locked Folder from the box.

Message

Messages enable the sending and receiving of text messages, photos, voice messages, and videos. You can get Messages from Google Play if you don't already have it.

Make Messages your default messaging app

If your smartphone has many messaging apps, you can make Messages the default. When you set Messages as your default messaging app, you can only send and receive new text messages from it, as well as view your text message history.

Select one of the choices below to make Messages your preferred messaging app:

1) Launch the Messages app.
2) When asked, change your default messaging app by following the on-screen instructions.

Alternatively:

1) Navigate to Settings.
2) Select Apps.
3) Click Messages, then SMS, and finally Messages from the list of apps.

How to Send & receive text & voice messages in Messages

Messages allow you to communicate with friends and contacts by sending and receiving text messages.

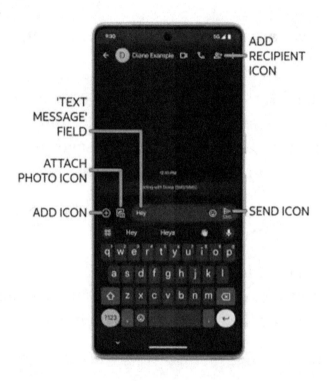

ADD RECIPIENT ICON

'TEXT MESSAGE' FIELD

ATTACH PHOTO ICON

ADD ICON

SEND ICON

Begin a conversation

1) Launch the Messages app.
2) Tap the Compose button.

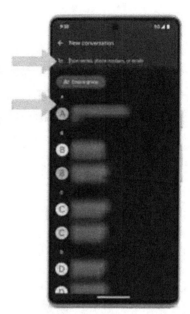

3) In "To," type the recipients' names, and contact information (phone or email), and message them. Additionally, you have the option to show your complete contact list or just your top contacts.

Send an email

1) Choose the message box.
2) Fill up the blanks with your message. Back Back to save it as a draft and come back to it later.

3) When you're done, click the Send button.

Send a voice message

1) Select the message box.
2) Select the Microphone option.
3) Make a recording of your voice message.
4) You can listen to the voice message before sending it by saving it as a draft.
5) The voice message is not sent until the Send Send button is pressed.
6) Choose Send.

Listen to voice message transcripts

You have the option to read a transcript or listen to a voice message when you receive one.

1) Launch the messaging app.
2) Click on the chat window from which you received the voicemail.
3) Select View Transcript located at the top of the voice message recording.

Forward a message

You can send a chat to a new contact at any time after you've started one.

1) Launch the Messages app.
2) Start a conversation.

3) Hold down a message.

4) Select more then go to forward.

5) Choose a contact.

6) Choose Send.

How to Read text messages

To view a new message, swipe down from the top of your screen and select New Message.

Mark all messages as read: Then tap More to mark everything as read.

Unread emails must be labeled as follows: Touch and hold the discussion in the conversation history that you want to mark as unread.

Tap More at the top, then mark it as unread.

Play the video or recording below: Create a recording of a chat. The Play button is located next to the video or recording.

Make a call: In the upper right corner, tap Call.

Read archived messages: From your list of topics, select More, then Archived.

How to Send photos, videos, or voice messages in Messages

Messages allow you to send and receive MMS content such as pictures, videos, audio files, and GIFs.

Send images, videos, files, or animated GIFs.

1) Launch the Messages app.
2) Start or open a chat.
3) Add a question by tapping Attach.
4) Choose a file.
5) Select Send.

Clean up conversations in Messages

You can archive outdated or undesirable discussions, designate all messages as read, or delete them from Messages.

1) Launch the Messages app.
2) Tap and hold each communication you want to save or delete.
   a) **Archive**: Tap Archive to add the selected chats to your archives. Archived chats are removed from the Home screen, although they can still be read.
   b) **Mark everything as read:** Then, tap More. Mark everything as read.
   c) **Delete:** Tap Delete to erase the chosen chats from Messages. Removed chats will be removed from your smartphone if you use Messages as your preferred messaging app. It is not possible to recover a deleted chat or message. This is a permanent action.

How to Block Someone in Messages

You can prohibit someone's communications in communications.

Block a conversation

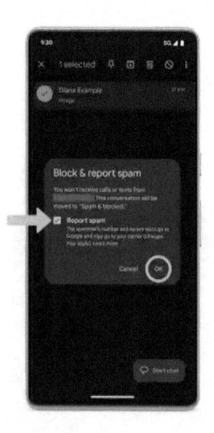

1) Launch the Messages app.
2) Tap and hold the chat you want to block on the Home screen.
3) Select "Block" and click OK.

Unblock a conversation

1) Launch the Messages app.
2) Select More then go to Spam and select Blocked.
3) Choose a contact from the list.

4) Unblock should be selected.
5) Otherwise, press the Back button.

How to Change Messages notifications & settings

When you receive a message, you have the option of being notified with a:

1) Sound
2) Vibration
3) Reminder

Change global settings

Modify your default messaging app.

1) Open the Settings app on your device.
2) Tap Apps, then Default Apps, and finally SMS App.

Change the font size.

1) Open your device's Settings app.
2) Choose Accessibility, then Text and Display.
3) Font size can be changed.
4) To change the font size, use the slider.

Change the size of the display

1) Open the Settings app on your device.
2) Choose Accessibility then Text and then Display Size of the display.
3) Select the display size using the slider.

Modify the advanced settings

Modify how Messages sends images, videos, and audio files.

1) Open the Messages app.
2) Tap More options, then Settings, and then Advanced.

Send a different message or file to each member in a discussion: Then, choose Group messaging. To receive individual responses, send an SMS message to all recipients (mass text).

Automatically download files from messages: Enable MMS auto-download.

When data roams, download files automatically: Enable Auto-download MMS while roaming.

Connectivity

How to Connect to Wi-Fi networks on your Pixel phone

To use WiFi as you see fit, you can change when and how your device connects to it.

Your device automatically connects to nearby Wi-Fi networks that you have already connected to when you turn on Wi-Fi. You can also configure your device to turn on Wi-Fi when it is close to a stored network.

How to Turn on & connect your wifi

1) Open the Settings app on your device.
2) Select Network & Internet
3) Turn on Wi-Fi.
4) Pick a network from the provided list. If a password is needed, the Lock will show up. After you connect, "Connected" appears beneath the network name.
5) The network was considered "saved." Your device connects right away if Wi-Fi is enabled and it is close by.

Connect via notification

You will be alerted to available, reliable public networks when you turn on Wi-Fi. The alerts are as follows:

1) Tap Connect to establish a network connection.
2) Tap All Networks to adjust the Wi-Fi settings.
3) Clear the notification to cease getting updates for that network.

Compare networks' strength

Strength

1) Open the Settings app
2) Choose the Internet & Network.
3) Verify that the Wi-Fi is working
4) The signal strength of the network is shown by the Wi-Fi symbol. A stronger signal is indicated by a larger symbol.

Speed

1) Open the Settings app on your phone.
2) Select Network & Internet, then the Internet.
3) Check that the Wi-Fi is turned on.
4) The connection speed is listed beneath the name of a public network. Signal strength influences speed.
   a) **Slow:** Emails and SMS can be sent and received.
   b) **OK:** you may browse the web, utilize social media, listen to music, and watch SD videos.
   c) **Fast:** It is possible to make video calls and stream the majority of high-definition (HD) videos.
   d) **Very fast:** You may stream videos of very high quality.

How to Change, add, share, or remove saved networks

Change a saved network

1) Open the Settings app.
2) Then, choose Network & Internet, then Wi-Fi.
3) To switch between networks, tap a name.
4) To change the network's settings, tap it.

Add an already saved network

1) Reload the network list.

Wait for the list to refresh if the network you want is nearby but not visible.

2) Include a network.
   a) Open the Settings app on your phone.
   b) Select Network & Internet, then the Internet.
   c) Check that the Wi-Fi is turned on.
   d) At the bottom of the list, tap Add Network.
   e) As needed, enter the network name (SSID) and security details.
   f) Save the file.

Share your Wi-Fi information with a friend

1) Open the Settings app
2) Select Network & Internet, then the Internet.
3) Check that the Wi-Fi is turned on.

4) Select a network, then Share.
5) A QR code will appear on your phone. Your friend can join the same network by scanning the code.

Remove a previously saved network

1) Open the Settings app
2) Select Network & Internet, then the Internet.
3) Check that the Wi-Fi is turned on.
4) Touch and hold a previously stored network.
5) Select Forget.

How to Connect to mobile networks on a Pixel phone

To change the way your phone uses data, adjust the settings on your mobile network.

Modify the mobile network settings

1) Open the Settings app on your phone.
2) Then select Network & Internet, followed by SIMs.
3) Select a setting by tapping it.
4) Open the Settings app on your phone, then select System, Advanced, and Reset to reset all of your network settings. Next, reset Bluetooth, mobile, and Wi-Fi.

How to Connect to a virtual private network (VPN) on Pixel phone

When you are not present, you can connect your device to a private network, such as the network at your school or workplace. A virtual private network (VPN) is used to establish this type of connection.

How to Use VPN by Google One
Turn on Google One VPN.

1) Open the Settings app.
2) Choose Network & Internet. Then VPN, then VPN by Google One.
3) Examine the disclosures and permissions requested.
4) If you agree, click the Use VPN button.

Stay private on VPN by Google One

Every time you connect to a network, the VPN connects automatically to further safeguard your privacy. Once the VPN is connected, the Key will appear at the top of your screen.

The VPN protects your data and online activities from hackers when using new internet providers or public Wi-Fi. This keeps you safe from apps and websites that use cookies to track where you are or what pages you visit.

To resume or suspend the VPN immediately, add the VPN by Google One tile to Quick Settings.

Pause VPN by Google One on the current network

1) Open the Settings app.
2) Choose Network & Internet. Then VPN, then VPN by Google One.
3) In the connection status panel, tap Pause VPN.

Use Quick Settings to pause VPN by Google One

To rapidly reach the pause settings, make the following tile:

1) Start Quick Settings.
2) Add the "VPN by Google One" tile.

Pause VPN by Google One automatically on a selected network

You can program the VPN to shut off automatically when using specific networks, like your mobile network.

1) Open the Settings app.
2) Choose Network & Internet. Then VPN, then VPN by Google One.

3) Choose the option to suspend VPN access on particular networks.
4) Press Add next to the network that you want to temporarily suspend the VPN for.

Exclude apps from Google One VPN

Google One VPN allows you to exclude specific apps. For example, if you don't want VPN latency to impair your game performance, you can disable multiplayer gaming. The VPN will no longer protect traffic added to this list of apps.

1) Open the Settings app.
2) Choose Network & Internet. Then VPN, then VPN by Google One.
3) Select Exclude selected apps.
4) Click Add next to the app you want to remove from the VPN.
5) To uninstall a particular app's traffic restriction from the VPN, go back to this screen and choose Trash.

How to Turn off VPN by Google One
To turn off the VPN, follow these steps:

1) Open the Settings app on your phone.
2) Select Network & Internet. Then VPN, followed by VPN by Google One.

3) Tap Use VPN to off.

How to Connect through Bluetooth on your Pixel phone

Some items can be connected to your phone over Bluetooth without the requirement of a wire. After the first time you pair a Bluetooth device, your devices may pair automatically. The top of the screen will display a Bluetooth icon if your phone is linked to anything through Bluetooth.

How to Turn Bluetooth on or off

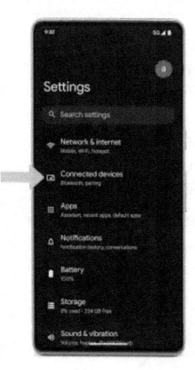 

1) Open the Settings app on your device.
2) Tap Connected Devices then Connection Preferences And then Bluetooth.
3) Turn Bluetooth on or off.

Option 1: Use the Settings app

1) Open the Settings app

2) Select Connected Devices. Then select Connection options, followed by Bluetooth. Check that Bluetooth is turned on. When you open the Bluetooth settings, adjacent devices can locate your device.

How To Pair a New Device.

Option 1: Tap the name of the Bluetooth device that you wish to pair with your phone.

Any on-screen instructions should be followed.

Option 2: Use notifications.

1) To begin pairing, turn on your Fast Pair accessory. Keep your accessory close to your smartphone or tablet.
2) When you receive a notification, tap to pair.
3) The "Device connected" or "Pairing complete" notification will appear.
4) If you need to configure your accessory, tap Set up now.
5) If you do not receive a notification, open your phone's settings app and select Connected Devices. Select the item you want to pair from the list of nearby devices.

Connect

1) Launch the Settings app.

2) Make sure Bluetooth is turned on.

3) Choose a device that is paired but not connected from the list.

4) When your devices are linked, the status is displayed as "Connected."

Configure, unpair, and rename a Bluetooth accessory.

1) Launch the Settings app on your device.

2) Navigate to the Bluetooth accessory's settings.

3) To access your accessory in the "Saved devices" section, tap the Settings icon next to its name.

4) If "Saved devices" does not show any accessories, tap the "See All" button. Select Settings next to the name of your item.

Make a Change

1) To change the name of an accessory, navigate to the top and select Edit setting, pencil icon.

2) To disconnect, use the Disconnect button.

3) Follow these steps to delete the device from your phone: Choose Forget.

How to Change the Bluetooth name on your phone.

1) Launch the Settings app.

2) Ensure Bluetooth is turned on.

3) Tap the device name.
4) Create a new name.
5) Select Rename.

How to share a mobile connection by tethering or hotspot

Use your phone's mobile data to connect another phone, tablet, or computer to the internet. Tethering, also known as hotspot use, is a method of sharing a connection.

Tether via Wi-Fi hotspot.

Use the Settings app.

Step 1: Turn on your phone's hotspot.

1) Launch the Settings app on your phone.
2) Choose Network & Internet, Hotspot & Tethering, and Wi-Fi hotspot.
3) Turn on your Wi-Fi hotspot.
4) View or update hotspot settings, such as name or password.

Step 2: Connect another device to your phone's hotspot.

1) Access the Wi-Fi settings menu on the other device.
2) Set a name for your phone's hotspot.

3) Enter the hotspot password using your phone.
4) Connect by clicking the button.

Use notifications.

Step 1: Confirm that your devices can use alerts to tether.

Step 2: Enable tethering using notifications.

1) Use the same account across devices.
2) Use the same Google account across all devices.
3) Enable Bluetooth and Wi-Fi.

Allow your phone to share its internet connection.

1) Launch the Settings app on your phone.
2) Tap Google, then Instant Tethering.
3) Enable the Provide data connection option.
4) Allow other devices to access your phone's internet connection.
5) Access the Settings app on your other device.
6) Tap Google, then Instant Tethering.
7) Enable the Get data connection option.

Step 3: Tether via notifications.

1) Configure all devices to tether via notifications, as previously discussed.
2) Have your phone with mobile data nearby.
3) Unlock the device you want to connect to